My Bible Story Collection

Adapted by Allia Zobel-Nolan

Illustrated by Trace Moroney

My Bible Story Collection
Copyright © 2003 Reader's Digest Children's Publishing, Inc.
Revised artwork © 2003 Trace Moroney

Published by Kregel Kidzone,
an imprint of Kregel Publications,
Grand Rapids, Michigan, 49501.

Manufactured in China.

10 9 8 7 6 5 4 3 2 1

My Bible Story Collection

This book belongs to

Contents

Introduction

The Bible is God's Word. It's like a big, long letter from him. It teaches us about his love and introduces us to his Son, Jesus.

There are lots of stories in the Bible. This book retells five of them. You'll see how God started this whole beautiful world with just a word. You'll sail along with Noah and his boat full of animals through the big flood. You'll discover what happened to Jonah when he disobeyed God, and more. You'll also find one of the Bible's best-loved stories—how God gave the world his only Son, Jesus, who was born over 2,000 years ago in a stable.

We hope these stories become some of your favorites and that you return to them again and again. We also hope this book will encourage you to read more of God's Word in your Bible.

When God Created the World

In the beginning, God created
the sky and the earth.

Genesis 1:1

8

In the beginning, there were no people. There was no sun to shine in the sky, and there were no stars to twinkle at night. There were no oceans, mountains, or valleys; no plants, trees, or flowers.

There was only God. So he decided to make everything. That's when he created Adam, the first man, and Eve, the first woman. But before Adam and Eve, God created. . .

. . .lots of animals! God made kangaroos with pockets and roly-poly elephants with long noses. God made lions that roar and insects that say, "katydid."

He made giraffes with long necks, zebras with striped coats, and tiny ladybugs with spotted backs. But before these, God created. . .

. . .birds to fill the sky. He made rainbow-colored parrots, flamingos with long, skinny legs, and woodpeckers that go *rat-a-tat-tat*.

God also made graceful swans with fuzzy-haired cygnets, horn-billed ducks, and white doves. But before these, God created. . .

. . .creatures for the ocean. God made sharks with
pointy teeth and whales that spout water high in the sky.

He made playful dolphins and wriggly-jiggly jellyfish.
But before that, God made. . .

. . .the sun for day and the moon for night. God also
dressed the night sky with sparkly lights he called stars.
But before that God created. . .

. . .plants, trees, and flowers. God made sunflowers that reach for the sky and teeny buttercups that giggle in the wind. God made trees with big red apples and fields of velvety grass.

God also gathered the water in one place to make the oceans and seas. The dry ground—deep valleys and rolling hills—he decided to call land. But before that God created. . .

. . .the big, blue sky. God decided it needed something else, so he filled it with white, fluffy clouds to hold

moisture, and clean, clear air to fill up the empty space. But before that God created. . . .

. . .light. God called that day. The dark, he called night. Before that, there was nothing. Only God was there.

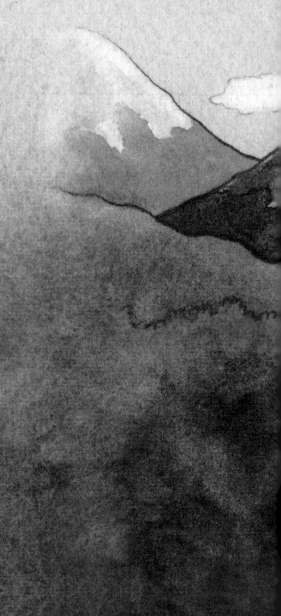

And it was oh, so quiet. That's when he turned on the light and started creating. And this is how it all began—in the beginning.

The Day
God Sent the Rain

God told Noah, "Build a big boat."
Then God told Noah to bring two of every animal and
his entire family aboard.

Genesis 6:14, 20

One day, God spoke to a man named Noah. "People have forgotten about me. They are doing bad things. So I'm sending rain to cover the earth. But I promise to keep you safe." Then God told Noah to build a very big boat.

So Noah sent for his three sons, and they all got to
work. They sawed wood, and they hammered in nails.
They made rooms and a great big door for the boat.
Then God told Noah about the animals.

"I'm sending you animals," God said. "Birds that fly, insects that crawl, giraffes with long necks, and elephants with big noses. I'm sending polar bears, and lions, and all sorts of living creatures," God said. "Take two of each on board."

Then God told Noah about the food. "Gather some of every kind and bring it with you. You're going to need it."

Drip, drop, drip, drop, drip, drop. God sent the rain. It came down softly but steadily. As it did, Noah's family made themselves at home on the ark. Then Noah went to check up on the animals.

"Don't worry," Noah told them. "Everything will be okay. God has promised to protect us. He'll keep us safe."

The rain continued. It fell faster and faster. Suddenly, without a word—BANG!—God shut the door. And still the rain poured down. Puddles grew, and the water rose higher and higher.

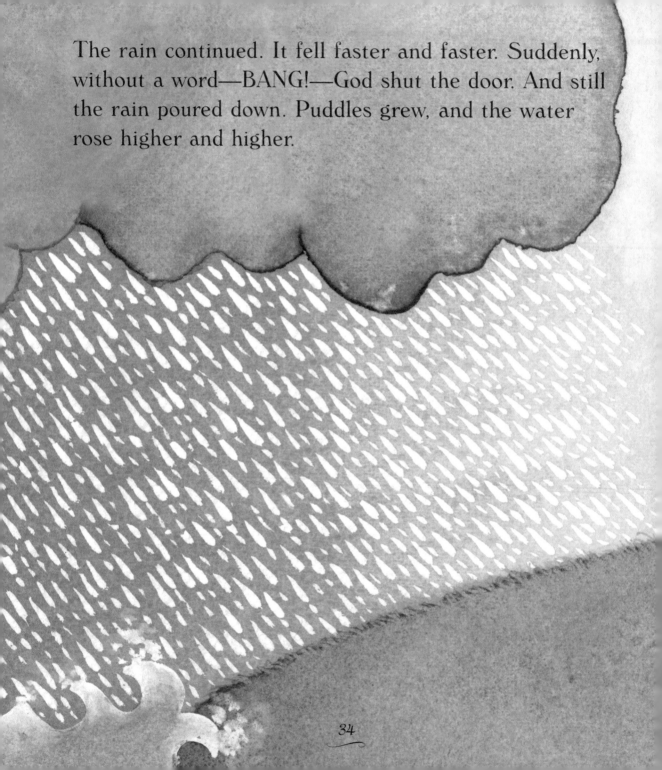

Noah, his family, and the animals waited. Soon the water covered the grass, the flowers, and even the trees. Then, all at once, the great big boat started to move. "Hold on," Noah said. "Here we go."

Lightning flashed and—KABOOM!—thunder roared. The ark rocked back and forth on the sea of rain. But God kept his promise. Noah and the animals were safe and sound.

The ark Noah had built was warm and dry, and there was plenty of food to eat. "When will the rain stop?" Noah's wife asked him. "When God wants it to," Noah replied.

37

Forty days came and went. Then one day, the sun began to shine. Noah went up on deck. Whales were playing tag and a strong wind was blowing. "The water will dry up soon," he said.

Days passed, and Noah sent a raven to look for land. The bird flew back quickly. "Nothing yet," Noah said to his wife. So they waited. Noah tried again—only this time he sent a dove.

The dove returned and flew over their heads. In its beak was a branch from an olive tree. Noah knew then that the ground was starting to dry. "Hurray," cried Noah and his family. The animals sniffed the fresh air and smiled.

"It won't be long now," Noah said. As the water continued to dry up, he began to see the tops of mountains. So he sent the dove out again, and this time, it did not return.

Meanwhile, the ark had come to a stop. Noah saw that the ground was dry. Then he heard God say, "Come out, now, Noah. Leave the ark." Noah thanked God for keeping his promise to protect everyone in the ark.

Then Noah looked up in the sky. "It's a rainbow," God said. "I put it in the sky as a sign of my love. It means I'll never flood the earth again." So Noah and his family and all the animals went their way, enjoying the green earth once again.

The Baby in the Basket

The baby's mother coated the basket with tar. Then she placed the child in it and sent it down the river.

Exodus 2:3–4

Once there was a woman who wanted to hide her baby from a mean king. So she made a basket that could float. Then she put her baby in it and went to the river.

"God, please keep my baby safe," she prayed.
After that, she placed the basket in the water
near the tall grass. "Stay here and see what
happens," she told her daughter.

Nearby at the palace, the king's daughter
was getting ready for a walk. "Let's go
bathe in the river," she said to her servants.

48

When they got to the water's edge, they
saw something floating near the tall grass.

"It looks like a basket," the princess said.
"Bring it here to me." So the princess'
servant walked into the water to get it.

The baby's sister peeked from behind the
bushes and held her breath. "God, please
save my brother," she whispered.

The princess opened the cover of the basket. The baby started crying. "There, there," she said, and she picked him up. As soon as she did, he smiled. It was then she knew she wanted to keep him. "I must find someone to care for him."

The baby's sister watched and listened. She heard the princess and quickly came up with a plan. "Thank you, God," she said as she stepped out from her hiding place.

The baby's sister acted quickly. She went up to the princess and said, "I know someone who can help you care for this baby."

The princess thought for a minute. Then she said,
"Go get her." So the girl ran home to get her mother.

"Mother! Mother!" she cried out when she reached the door.
"Something wonderful has happened. God has heard our
prayer." The woman stopped working and listened while her

daughter explained all that had happened. She whispered a
prayer of thanks as her daughter grabbed her hand. "We
must go quickly," the girl said.

So the woman took care of the baby for the princess.
And she was very happy. God had not only kept her baby

safe, but he also saw to it that she would care for him. The princess named the baby Moses.

Jonah and the Big Fish

The Lord provided a great fish to swallow Jonah.

Jonah 1:17

"Go to Nineveh," God told Jonah one day. "The people are doing bad things. Tell them to change or

I will have to punish them." But Jonah didn't obey.
He didn't like the Ninevites. They were enemies of
God's people. So he packed his bags and ran away.

He went to the dock and bought a ticket for a ship. It was headed to a distant city. Jonah thought he could hide from God there.

Now, the sailors didn't know what Jonah had done.
So they took him on board and set sail. Jonah felt
safe on the ship.

But God knew exactly where Jonah was. And he sent a storm to teach him a lesson. "Why is this happening?" the sailors cried out. "Jonah," they shouted, "ask your God to save us!"

Now, Jonah knew he was to blame. He should not have disobeyed God. "The storm is my fault," he told the others. "Throw me overboard," he begged, "and it will stop."

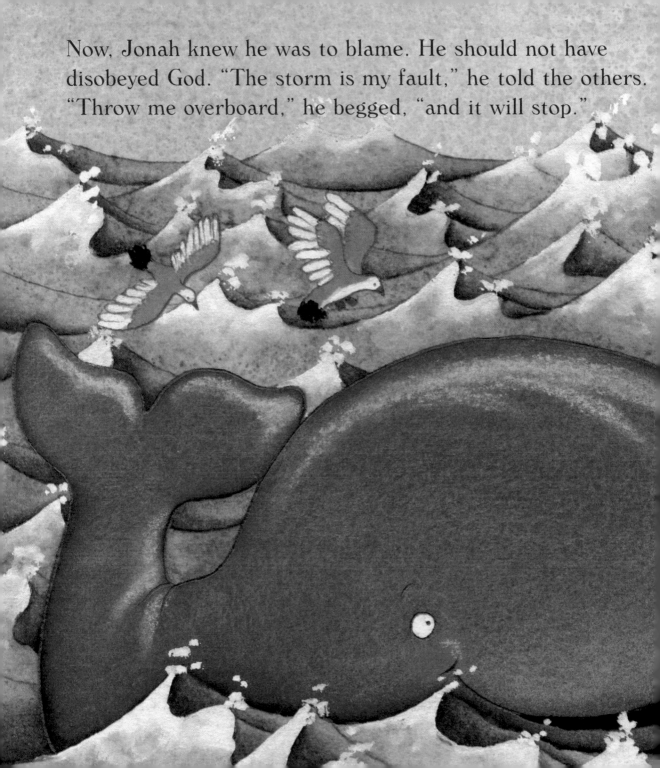

The sailors didn't think what Jonah asked them to do was right. But then the boat started to sink. So they picked Jonah up and—*splash*—tossed him into the sea.

When they did, the wind quieted and the water started to calm. They watched as Jonah bobbed up and down in the waves. Then, suddenly, the biggest fish they had ever seen

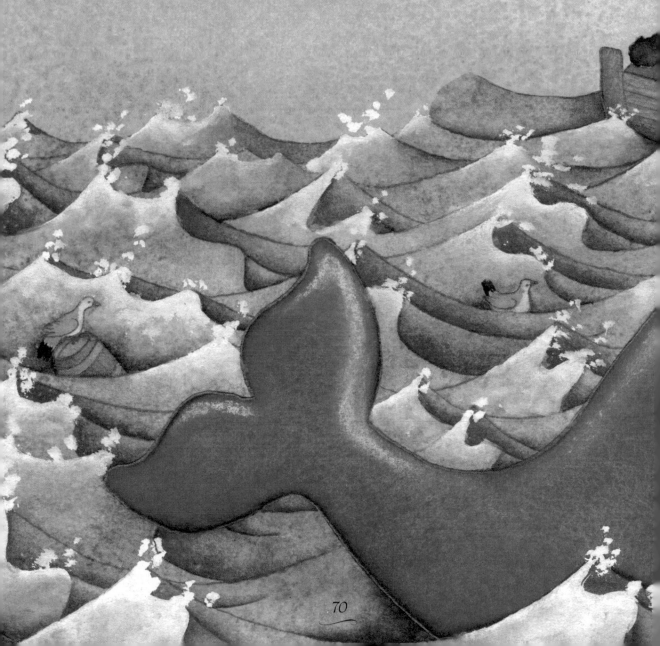

rose up and—*gulp*—swallowed Jonah. The sailors were sad. They didn't realize this was what God had planned. He had sent the fish to rescue Jonah from drowning.

Jonah slid deep down into the belly of the fish.
There, he knelt and prayed. "Lord, I thank you

for sending this fish to save me. Can you ever forgive me for not obeying you?"

God heard Jonah's prayers and gave him another chance.
He told the fish to swim near the beach and spit Jonah out.

So, the fish did as it was told, and the next thing Jonah knew, he had landed on the shore.

A few days passed, and God said to Jonah again, "Go to Nineveh and give the people my message." And this time, Jonah went. He preached to the men and women there, and they stopped doing wrong. God saw how the people had changed and did not punish them after all.

One Night in Bethlehem

Mary will give birth to a son, and they
will call him Immanuel, which means,
"God is with us."

Matthew 1:23

78

God sent an angel to a girl named Mary. "I have good news," he said. "God has picked you to have a special baby. He will be God's Son."

Mary was surprised and afraid. But she
trusted God. So she answered the angel,
"I'll do whatever God wants."

Soon after, Mary and Joseph, her husband, heard a soldier read a new law from the ruler, Caesar. "Everyone must return to the place where he was born to be counted," the soldier said

Now, Joseph's family came from Bethlehem, a town seventy miles away. "We'd better leave today," Joseph said. Mary nodded.

Joseph helped Mary onto their donkey and walked beside her. They joined others who were making the same journey.

The trip seemed endless, and Mary longed for a soft bed. It was almost time for her baby to be born and she was weary.

When they arrived in Bethlehem, Joseph looked for a place to stay. But everywhere he checked, all the rooms were taken

Finally, a kind innkeeper said, "You can sleep in my stable. At least there you'll have shelter." So that's what Mary and Joseph did.

And that night, Mary's baby boy, Jesus, was born. While the animals looked on, Mary wrapped her newborn child in cloths and put him in the dry hay of the manger.

At the same time, shepherds in a nearby field were looking after their sheep when angels filled the sky. The shepherds were terrified.

"Don't be afraid," one of the angels said. "Tonight, Jesus, God's Son, is born in Bethlehem. You'll find him in a stable. Go now and look for him."

The shepherds ran to see if what the angels said was true. They searched everywhere until they came to the stable. When they looked in, they saw the baby. "His name is Jesus," Mary said, and the shepherds fell on their knees. "Here is our Savior," they said. "We have found God's Son."

For to us a child is born, to us a Son is given,
and he will be called Wonderful Counselor,
Mighty God, Prince of Peace.

Isaiah 9:6